OCCASIONAL CONTRIBUTIONS FROM THE MUSEUM OF ANTHROPOLOGY OF THE UNIVERSITY OF MICHIGAN
NO. 5

PERFORATED INDIAN CRANIA IN MICHIGAN

BY
W. B. HINSDALE and EMERSON F. GREENMAN

ANN ARBOR, MICHIGAN
UNIVERSITY OF MICHIGAN PRESS
August 15, 1936

ISBN (print): 978-1-949098-58-7
ISBN (ebook): 978-1-951538-58-3

Browse all of our books at
sites.lsa.umich.edu/archaeology-books.

Order our books from the University of Michigan
Press at www.press.umich.edu.

For permissions, questions, or manuscript queries, contact Museum publications by email at umma-pubs@umich.edu or visit the Museum website at lsa.umich.edu/ummaa.

FOREWORD

This paper is an account by Dr. Hinsdale of a preliminary archaeological survey in eastern Michigan. He recognized the significance of the first reports of the sites and by trips to them during the summer of 1934 verified the evidence. The following winter was devoted by him to compiling from many bibliographic sources the comparative data contained in these pages. His persistent inquiry into the problem has focused attention upon the cultural significance of perforated Indian crania found in the region of the Great Lakes. Owing in large measure to his interest in the work a fund for the study of Michigan Indian history has been established, by means of which intensive excavations at the Younge site in Lapeer County were undertaken during the summer of 1935. Dr. Greenman has collaborated with Dr. Hinsdale by assembling a portion of the references, and by arranging the text for this series.

The publication of this number of the *Occasional Contributions from the Museum of Anthropology* has been made possible by a grant from the Horace H. Rackham and Mary A. Rackham Fund.

C. E. G.

PERFORATED INDIAN CRANIA IN MICHIGAN

DURING the summer of 1934 three accidentally discovered aboriginal sites in southeastern Michigan were investigated for the Division of the Great Lakes, Museum of Anthropology.[1] In each location where digging was done crania were unearthed in which small holes had been drilled. The operations had been performed after death. Upon no other occasion in twelve years of rather intensive and of thirty years of periodical investigation in nearly every county in the Lower Peninsula and in four counties in the Upper Peninsula has this feature been discovered, although others have described perforated skulls from places remote from one another and from the sites reported in this account.

While in modern surgery any intentional instrumental opening into a skull is usually termed a trephination, a distinction between trephination and perforation may be made for the purposes at hand. The holes in the crania to be described are made as if countersunk and vary in greatest diameters from nine to ten millimeters. The operations appear to have been performed by drilling, and, consequently, the parts of the bone coming away were like dust, or similar to filings and scrapings, whereas in most instances of trephining a disk of bone is removed. The so-called trephined skulls that have previously come to light in Michigan have circular openings (Pl. I, Fig. 1). Those to be discussed are

[1] The Younge site, Goodland Township, Lapeer County, was discovered by Mr. Carman Baggerly in 1934 and brought to the attention of the Museum by Dr. C. M. Braidwood of Imlay City. The graves at the Farmington site, Farmington Township, Oakland County, were accidentally discovered in the summer of 1934, and notice of them was given at once to the Museum by Roy N. Reynolds, the sheriff of Oakland County. The site near Flat Rock, Huron Township, Wayne County, was discovered in 1934 by Harry Hosack.

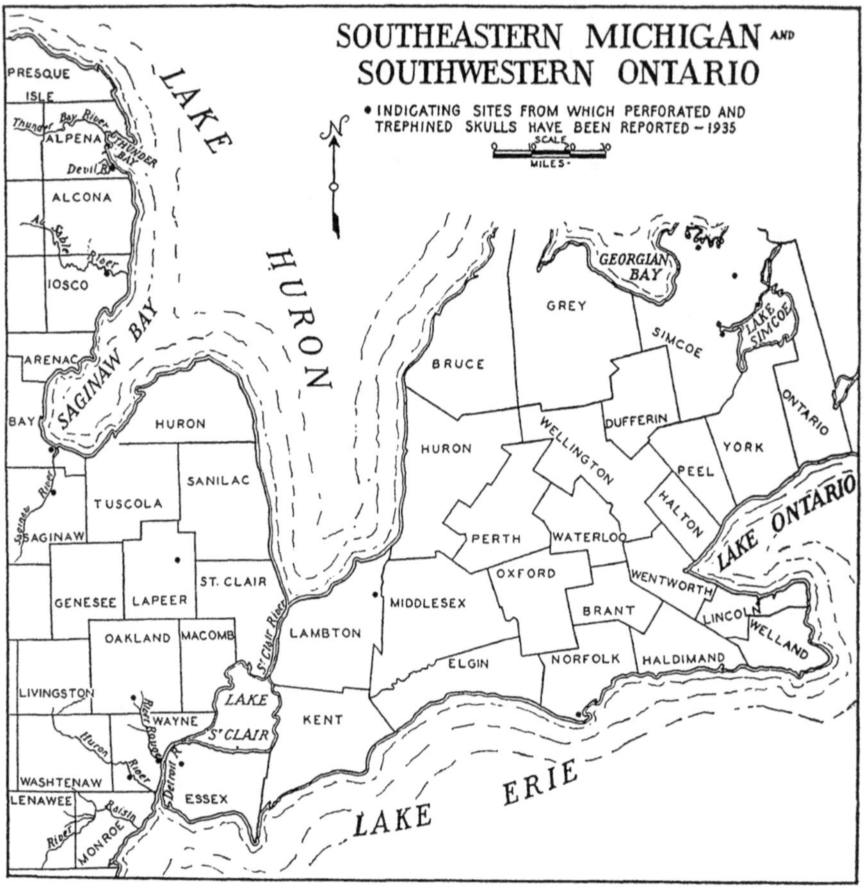

MAP 1. The trephined calvarium in Plate I, Figure 1 was taken from a mound at the site in Alpena County, Michigan. A cranium with a hole 2 cm. in diameter was found in a mound at the site indicated in Iosco County, Michigan. This was probably another trephination. Crania with one or more holes drilled after death were found on the remainder of the sites indicated.

also circular and as if countersunk, with a difference of two or three millimeters in inner and outer diameters. The term *perforation* will be used in reference to this type of hole.

The perforations in the crania found in Michigan are either immediately in front of or behind bregma, and in only two instances has more than one perforation been observed in a single specimen. All but one of the five crania in the Museum are somewhat fragmentary, and all but one represent adults. Since all specimens observed or in possession of the Museum were not excavated by members of the staff, complete details *in situ* cannot be given.

The three sites under discussion are north, west, and south of Detroit in the southeastern part of the state. The first is near the village of Flat Rock, twenty miles south of Detroit, in Huron Township, Wayne county, just over the western boundary of the former Wyandot Indian Reservation, according to a map made by Douglas Houghton, published in 1840. At this site four of twenty crania were perforated at the vertex. Two of these, both of adults, were secured by the Museum. One, consisting of the frontal bone with adjacent portions of both parietals, has the perforation about 15 mm. anterior to bregma, in median position. The outer diameter is 1 cm., the inner is 6 mm. (Pl. I, Fig. 2).[2] The other cranium has the bones of the face and the right supraorbital missing. The perforation is in the frontal bone, 2 cm. anterior to bregma in median position. The hole deviates a little from the circular with a greatest (transverse) diameter of 9 mm. on the outside. The inner end is more nearly circular, with a diameter of 6 mm. Between bregma and lambda a roughly circular portion of this cranium involving about equal halves of the two parietals is missing, apparently the result of the removal of a disk. The hole is about 10 cm. in diameter, one edge passing through lambda and the other through a point 1.4 cm. posterior to bregma.

[2] Catalogue No. 4346.

The uneven character of the edges would suggest a crushing blow as the cause of the hole if it were not for the presence of an incision about a centimeter long, made by a cutting edge, close to the rim of the hole. There are shallow scratches on both parietal bones just below and behind the parietal tuberosities, also on the right parietal and temporal bones in the region of the suture separating the two (Pl. II).[3]

Five crania, entire and in good condition, were found near the village of Farmington, about fifteen miles west of Detroit. At this place the skeletal remains of about seventeen individuals were encountered in a commercial gravel pit within a space fifteen feet long, eight feet wide, and five feet deep. All of these crania are perforated at the vertex and one, in possession of the Museum,[4] has in addition another hole in the base just back of the foramen magnum. The perforation at the top of this one is 1 cm. back of bregma and across the sagittal suture. The diameters are 9 mm. (outer) and 8 mm. (inner). The hole in the base is less symmetrical and may have been made by other than a human agency (Pl. III, Figs. 1-2).

There are also perforations in long bones from the Farmington site. Two femurs and two tibiae are perforated near the ends.[5] Although dissociated from any other parts of a skeleton they apparently belonged to the same individual and were lying in normal articulation. A hole 5 mm. in diameter is in the distal end of the shaft of the left femur, antero-posterior. A hole in similar position on the anterior surface of the right femur was carried only to a depth of about 1 cm. The drill was started in the opposite surface of the femur to meet this hole but was only carried to a depth of about 1 mm. Another hole had been started in the anterior surface at the other end of this femur, at the distal

[3] Catalogue No. 4347. See Appendix for measurements of this cranium.
[4] Catalogue No. 4348.
[5] Catalogue No. 4392.

end of the neck. It is 8 mm. deep. Both femurs have the heads cut so that each head is a disk about 23 mm. wide. At the other ends both condylar surfaces are missing, apparently they were severed (Pl. IV, Fig. 1).

The perforations in the two tibiae are at the proximal ends. Both articular surfaces have been cut off, and both anterior borders have been shaved down 1 or 2 cm. distal to the tuberosities. The distal ends have also been cut, but the greater part of each articular surface remains. There are two holes through the proximal end of each tibia, one antero-posterior and the other lateral, so that originally they may have intersected in the interior of the shafts, where cancellous tissue has now fallen away. The holes are from 6 to 7 mm. in diameter. The hole in the external surface of the left tibia could not have been more than 7 mm. deep. On the external-lateral surface of this tibia, from the anterior border down to the nutrient foramen, there is a scratch that may have been made with a flint knife.

Of eight or ten crania from the site on the Roy Younge farm in Lapeer County, about sixty miles north of Detroit, five were perforated at the vertex. Two of these were obtained for the Museum. One is the frontal bone of a child of seven or eight years, with the perforation 4 mm. anterior to bregma in median position (Pl. IV, Fig. 2). The diameters are 9 mm. (outside), and 8 mm. (inside). The bone is only 2.5 mm. thick.[6] The other skull, which is in a fragmentary condition, was part of a bundle burial of an adult. The perforation, 8 mm. back of bregma through the sagittal suture, has an outside greatest (transverse) diameter of 12 mm., and an inner greatest (transverse) diameter of 7 mm. A disk has been removed from the posterior portion of the cranium, involving about equal portions of the parietal bones, with a resulting hole 5 cm. in diameter.[7]

[6] Catalogue No. 4339.
[7] Catalogue No. 4675.

Another pair of leg bones lying in the correct relationship to one another and dissociated from other parts of a skeleton, was found at the Younge site. It was part of a burial in which the remains of at least two individuals were accompanied by the skulls of two bears (Text Figure 1).

In 1875 Henry Gillman described about twenty crania with holes from one-third to three-quarters of an inch in diameter; he stated that the holes had been made after death by drilling.[8] The crania were from four sites, the so-called

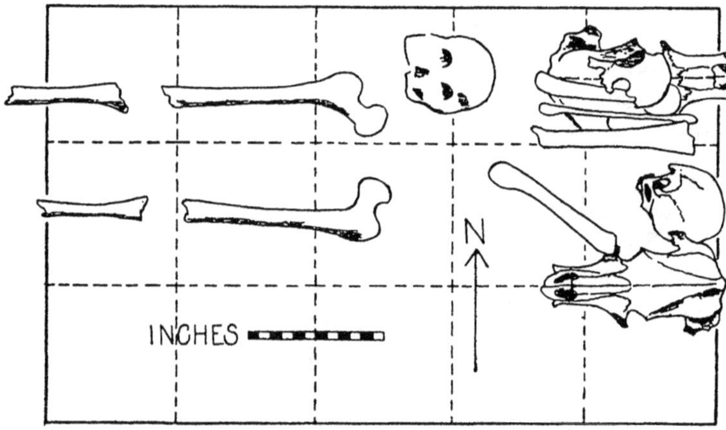

FIG. 1

Great Mound on River Rouge, at Springwells, Wayne County, near Detroit, a mound on Sable (now Au Sable) River near Alpena, a mound on Devil River in the same general part of the state, and a mound near Saginaw. The data for most of these crania are unsatisfactory, however, leaving only two that are sufficiently well described for the purposes of the present discussion.[9] Both

[8] Henry Gillman, "Certain Characteristics pertaining to Ancient Man in Michigan," *Ann. Rept. Smithsonian Institution*, 1875, 234-245.

[9] A calvarium from Devil River mound (Pl. I, Fig. 1) now in the Museum, which was included by Gillman in his description of crania with drilled perforations, has been identified as a trephination, accomplished during life (see W. B. Hinsdale, *Primitive Man in Michigan*, Michigan Handbook Series, No. 1 (1925), 128, Fig. 2). Another cranium from a mound on

were taken from the Great Mound on River Rouge. The perforation was at bregma on one (Gillman's No. 1), and two-tenths of an inch back of bregma on the other (Gillman's No. 6. See Text Figure 2). The diameter of the first, as inferred from the actual size illustration, was between 7 mm. and 14 mm.; of the other, about one-third of an inch (8 mm.), as stated in the text. Four skulls with holes in them were taken from the Great Mound, two fragments in 1869 and two more in 1874. It can only be surmised that the two not described in detail by Gillman had drilled perforations.[10]

Another perforated cranium was found near Bay City in 1903. According to a contemporary notice in a New York

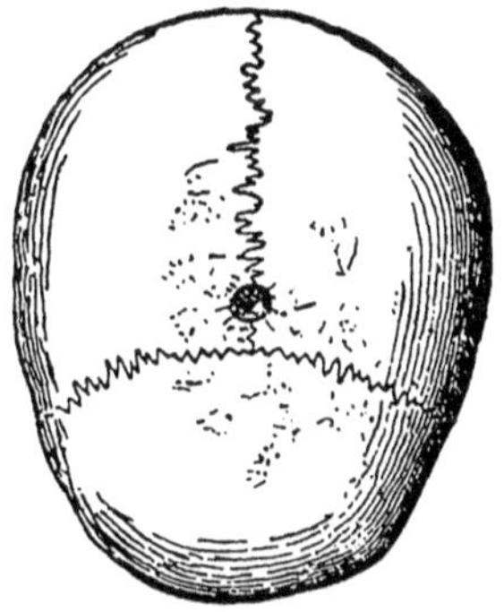

FIG. 2

newspaper the site was an artificial mound,[11] but the following information is on the card accompanying this specimen in an exhibition case in the American Museum of Natural History:

> E. H. Crane. Purchase 1903—No. 7 from Mr. E. H. Crane. No. 20/8098. 1 perforated skull, from a skeleton found about 3

Au Sable River has a round hole about 2 cm. in diameter half way between lambda and bregma on the sagittal suture. The size and position of the hole suggest another trephination for this cranium as well as the ten or fifteen others from this mound described by Gillman as similarly perforated. The cranium from the mound at Saginaw is described as having three perforations at the apices of a triangle.

[10] See Appendix for measurements of the crania described by Gillman.

[11] *The New York Sun*, March 13, 1903.

miles above West Bay City, Michigan, in a depression at foot of a sand ridge, the ridge was a burial place. Found by M.C.R.R. on R.R. property while laying water pipe and 2 feet above high water mark. Stone arrow points were found in the grave.

The perforation is a short distance in front of bregma.

There is another cranium in possession of the Museum which was received some years ago from the University of Michigan Medical School (Pl. V). This skull has two holes at the vertex of about the same size and shape as those that have been described. A hole occurs in each parietal bone about 1 cm. both from the sagittal and coronoid sutures. A portion of the bone between the two perforations is missing, but it has been restored in the illustration. The origin of this cranium is not known.[12]

Through correspondence and search in the literature it becomes apparent that crania with perforations similar to those from Michigan have been found in the United States only in regions adjoining the State on the south and east. Closest of these to southeastern Michigan, and separated from it by the Detroit River, are several sites in Ontario, Canada, between the southeastern curve of Georgian Bay and Lake Simcoe, in Norfolk County near the shore of Lake Erie, in Lambton County, and in the city of Windsor directly across from Detroit. Out of a total of twelve crania that are described in more or less detail, seven bear a single perforation. One of these is from Innisfil, Simcoe County. The hole is described as drilled, and has a diameter of 7 mm.; the illustration given places it just ahead of bregma in median position.[13] Another cranium was found in an ossuary containing the remains of some hundreds of individuals in Oro Township, Simcoe County. It is described as having "a

[12] Catalogue No. 4343. A label pasted on the forehead is inscribed: "Indian of Michigan, Dr. S. Lathrop."

[13] David Boyle, "Notes on Some Specimens," *Ann. Archaeol. Rept., 1899, Ontario.* 1900, 26, Figs. 13-14.

circular perforation on the top resembling a bullet-hole."[14] The remaining five crania were found in a Windsor cemetery in the summer of 1935 by W. J. Wintemberg of the National Museum of Canada. They have been briefly described, as follows:

> Several bundle burials, surrounded by skulls, and two torso burials were discovered. Five of the skulls have a hole drilled through the sagittal suture near the bregma, and another has a lenticular cut, about 3 inches long and ⅜-inch wide (apparently made by sawing with a knife of chipped stone) which extends transversely across the parietals and penetrates the brain cavity. One of the bundles of long-bones included an artificially perforated humerus and femur.[15]

The rest of these Canadian specimens that are described in detail have from two to six holes each. Of two from an ossuary near Akrona, Lambton County, Ontaria, one has six and the other three holes in the parietal bones at and near the top.[16] A second cranium from the ossuary at Innisfil, Simcoe County, has three holes with diameters of half an inch. These holes, however, were cut rather than drilled. The holes are at, and on either side, of bregma.[17] Mr. Wintemberg has described two more specimens in correspondence:

> Two perforated skulls from single graves on a site of the same culture as the Uren Village Site (*Bulletin* 51, National Museum of Canada), on lot 7, concession A, South Walsingham Township, Norfolk County. One of them with three holes is in the National Museum of Canada, Catalogue No. VIII-F-18998. The other, a fragment of the top of a skull, with two perforations is in the Norfolk Museum, Simcoe, Ontario. The site is pre-European.

[14] Andrew F. Hunter, "Notes on Sites of Huron Villages in the Township of Oro, Simcoe County, Ontario," *Ann. Archaeol. Rept., 1902, Ontario.* 1903, 174.

[15] "Notes and News," *Am. Antiquity*, I, No. 3 (1936), 232.

[16] David Boyle, "Bored Skulls," *Ann. Archaeol. Rept. 1903, Ontario.* 1904, 91-92, Figs. 61-62.

[17] David Boyle, *op. cit.* (1899), 26, Figs. 13-14.

There are still other perforated crania from Canadian sites for which the number and position of the holes are not definitely stated. Hunter[18] mentions "two or three skulls with round holes in them," from an ossuary in Simcoe County at the foot of a hill "against the face of which the abandoned beaches of the Great Nipissing Lake are strongly marked." Finally, Wintemberg states in correspondence that "a number of skulls from a post-European Huron ossuary in the town of Barrie, Vespra Township, Simcoe County, had round holes in the forehead."

Next in proximity to the Michigan sites containing perforated crania are two of the major mound groups of the Hopewell culture in southern Ohio. Moorehead[19] describes a post-morten perforation near the foramen magnum of a cranium from a mound of the Hopewell Group near Chillicothe, Ohio. The illustration shows the hole to be circular, and it is stated that the diameter of it is "perhaps three millimeters." Shetrone[20] describes another cranium from the same mound group with a perforation also in the occiput; he definitely states that it was drilled. Each of these crania lay beside a complete skeleton. Shetrone notes further that in Mound 7 of the Hopewell Group a cranium which was apparently unaccompanied by other bones had a disk removed from the occipital region:

> The occipital bone has been removed, apparently cut by a flint implement, and somewhat ground off along the resulting edges.[21]

In Mound 3 of the Turner Group near Cincinnati[22] six perforated skulls were part of a group of sixteen detached

[18] Andrew F. Hunter, "Notes on Sites of Huron Villages in the Township of Tay (Simcoe County)," *Am. Archaeol. Rept., 1899, Ontario*. 1900, 70.

[19] Warren K. Moorehead, *Primitive Man in Ohio*. New York: G. P. Putnam's Sons, 1892. P. 234.

[20] H. C. Shetrone, "Exploration of the Hopewell Group of Earthworks," *Ohio Archaeol. and Hist. Quarterly*, XXXV, No. 1 (1926), 93.

[21] *Ibid.*, 38.

[22] C. C. Willoughby and E. A. Hooton, "The Turner Group of Earthworks, Hamilton County, Ohio," *Papers Peabody Mus. Am. Archaeol. and* Ethnol., VIII, No. 3 (1922), 60-61, 124-125.

skulls placed at regular intervals around two extended skeletons at the bottom of a pit which had been dug down from the surface of the mound. Thirteen of the skulls have scratches, as if made by a flint knife in removing the flesh. One cranium has a single hole, in the left parietal bone, "46 mm. back of the coronal suture, and 30 mm. external to the sagittal suture," and in the remainder there is more than one hole, the diameters ranging from 3 mm. to 9 mm. Another skull with a perforation near the great foramen was found in Marriott Mound 1 of the Turner Group, "unaccompanied by other bones." The hole is one-quarter of an inch in diameter, and was bored through the occipital bone near the margin of the foramen magnum.[23] It may be noted that near-by there were two skeletons which were "out of natural order."

Cut sections of human skulls, unperforated or with one or more perforations, have been found in lower Canada, in Ohio, and in New York. Two round disks from eastern Ontario perforated with several holes have in addition groups of paired incised lines.[24] Mound 7 of the Hopewell Group yielded, in addition to the cranium already described, two fragments of parietal bone with drilled holes one-eighth of an inch in diameter; [25] and a round disk three and one-fourth inches in diameter, cut from a human skull and bearing two perforations near the edge, was found unassociated with other remains in the Westenhaver Mound, Ross County, Ohio.[26] From Jefferson County, New York, is reported a disk about four inches in diameter, with nine apparently drilled perforations.[27] Of two others from the same

[23] *Ibid.*, 61, 88.

[24] David Boyle, "Notes on Some Specimens," *Ann. Archaeol. Rept., 1902, Ontario.* 1903, 30-31, Figs. 11–12.

[25] H. C. Shetrone, *op. cit.*, 38.

[26] William C. Mills, "Explorations of the Westenhaver Mound," *Ohio Archaeol. and Hist. Publications,* XXVI, No. 2 (1917), 257, Fig. 15.

[27] William M. Beauchamp, "Horn and Bone Implements of the New York Indians," *New York State Mus. Bull.*, 50 (1902), 335, Pl. 13.

locality, one has four perforations approximately at the corners of a square, and the other is unperforated.[28]

The facts brought out in the foregoing discussion may be simplified in the following summary: crania with a single perforation at the vertex, drilled after death, have been found at four sites in southeastern Michigan and at three sites in western Ontario; crania with more than one perforation, or with an unknown number, have been found at one site in Michigan, at seven in Ontario, and at two in Ohio. Circular disks cut from human crania and perforated with two or more holes, are found in Ohio, Ontario, and New York.

The seven sites in Michigan and Ontario yielding crania with a single perforation have other features in common. On all but the Flat Rock site (south of Detroit) there were signs that skulls had been separated from the other bones of skeletons, either by lack of other bones, or by the fact of their occurrence in an ossuary. At the Farmington site, as already described, possibly at the Great Mound on River Rouge,[29] at Windsor, and near Simcoe, Ontario,[30] certain long bones were perforated. Although all four of the Michigan sites were sandy, blue clay, mixed with varying amounts

[28] A. B. Skinner, "Notes on Iroquois Archaeology," *Mus. Am. Indian, Heye Foundation,* No. 18 (1921), 137-138, Pl. XXIII.

[29] Gillman, *op. cit.*, 234-238, Figs. 1-2. Two humeri, perforated at the olechranon processes, are discussed. Gillman regards these as natural perforations, but in the accompanying drawings the holes appear to be cut.

[30] "In a gravel-pit near the town of Simcoe were found the lower thirds of two human femurs, and the whole of a tibia, each of which is bored as seen in the illustrations. The other fragmentary femur is not shown, because it corresponds in every particular with the one represented here, except that it is a little shorter. In the tibia . . . it will be observed that three holes are bored side by side, and in line . . . Along with these there were an eyed bone needle of the usual type and a foreign shell (a species of *Natica* also bored) the two being attached by a strand of hair." David Boyle, *op. cit.*, 1892, 49, Figs. 75-76. In the drawings the holes are about one-half an inch in diameter. On the femur illustrated (Fig. 75), near the apex of the popliteal space, there is a single bored hole. On the tibia (Fig. 76) there are three holes in the line of the main axis of the bone, not more than 1 or 2 mm. apart, at what appears to be the distal end of the shaft.

of sand, covered the bones of the face of the perforated crania from Farmington, from the Younge site, and from Flat Rock. Paired extended skeletons with heads in opposite directions were found at Flat Rock and at the Younge site. The fact that all of the Michigan sites were sandy[31] is significant in itself. In addition, the site near Arkona, Ontario, is definitely described as sandy, and the sandy character of that in Tay Township, Simcoe County, Ontario, may safely be assumed from its description as very close to the abandoned beach of glacial Lake Nipissing.

The similarities between the Michigan-Ontario sites and those to the south in Ohio are not such as to suggest any direct, intimate relationship. This is to be expected, for the northern sites are open villages or cemeteries, while those in Ohio are all burial mounds. The greatest correspondence between these groups, aside from perforation itself, is in the association between perforation and disarticulation of crania. Lack of details concerning the two mounds in Michigan where perforated crania were found prohibits any comparison with those of Ohio.

No material of European manufacture has been found on any of the Michigan sites, but those in Oro, Vespra, and Tay townships, Simcoe County, Ontario, are described as post-European.

From the foregoing it is apparent that there is sufficient evidence of a specific culture trait complex in a restricted region to warrant further intensive study in the attempt to determine its associations. The field work of the Division of the Great Lakes in 1935, at the Younge site in Lapeer County, Michigan, was in continuance of this project. A report on it is in preparation.

[31] The so-called Great Mound on River Rouge near Detroit, Michigan, was not a true burial mound, but rather a natural sandy ridge which had been heightened in places by addition of earth to cover burials. See W. B. Hinsdale, *op. cit.*, 39.

APPENDIX

The following observations and measurements of crania were made by Dr. C. E. Guthe and Dr. M. Titiev.

Catalogue No. 4348. Calvaria, poor condition. Male. Medium muscularity. Middle-aged adult (36-55). Artificial lambdoid deformation pronounced. Brow ridges large, divided. Glabella large. Very low, medium sloping frontal region; bosses small. Bosses of parietal region small-medium. Temporal region medium fullness. Occipital region pronounced curve; inion large. Pronounced lambdoid flattening. No external occlusion. Large glenoid fossa depth. Oval auditory meatus. Elliptical shaped orbits, pronounced inclination. Deep suborbital fossa. Very large malars, large lateral and anterior projection. Pronounced thickness of zygomatic process. Nasion depression small. Nasal root high, large breadth. Nasal bridge height medium, breadth medium. Concave nasal profile. Mid-facial prognathism absent.

CRANIAL MEASUREMENTS

	mm.	
Glabello-occipital length	175	
Maximum width	135	
Basion-bregma height	136	
Minimum frontal diameter	92	
Bizygomatic diameter	135	(estimate)
Nasion-prosthion height	62	
Basion-nasion length	102	
Basion-prosthion length	89	
Nasal height	57	
Nasal breadth	27	
Orbital height—left	33	
Orbital breadth—left	42	
Orbital height—right	34	
Orbital breadth—right	40	
Interorbital breadth	22	
Biorbital breadth	100	

INDICES

Cranial	77.3
Height-length	77.3
Height-breadth	100.0
Nasal	49.0
Left orbital	80.5

Catalogue No. 4347. Cranial measurements: length, 195 mm.; breadth, 143 mm. Cranial index 73.

In the following table are the measurements (in inches and cubic inches) given by Gillman[32] for the two crania from the Great Mound.

	No. 1	No. 6
Capacity	18.65	18.23
Length	7.30	6.80
Breadth	6.00	5.80
Height	5.35	5.63
Breadth of frontal	4.02	4.63
Latitudinal index	0.822	0.853
Altitudinal index	0.733	0.828
Index of foramen magnum	0.465	0.397
Frontal arch	12.15	11.10
Parietal arch	12.00	13.15
Occipital arch	11.65	11.00
Longitudinal arch	14.00	14.85
Length of frontal	5.50	5.40
Length of parietal	4.40	4.60
Length of occipital	4.10	4.85
Zygomatic diameter	......	5.60
Circumference	19.00	24.40

[32] *Op. cit.*, 244.

PLATE I

FIG. 1. Trephination near vertex of calvarium from Devil River Mound, Michigan.

FIG. 2. Post-mortem, drilled perforation in fragment of a cranium from near Flat Rock, Wayne County, Michigan.

PLATE I

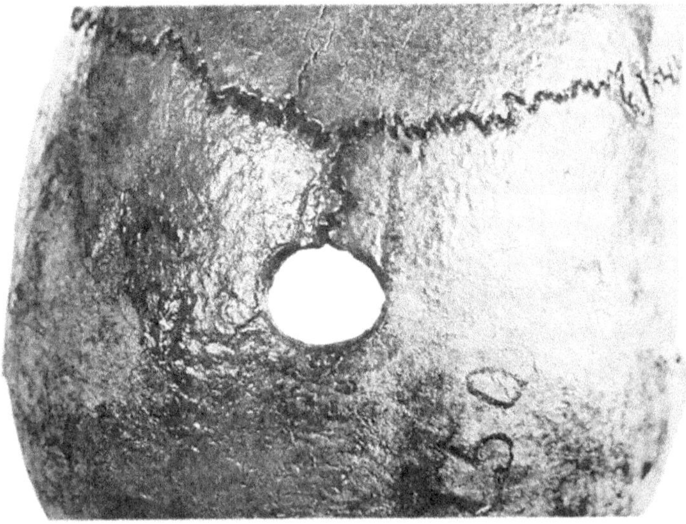

FIG. 1

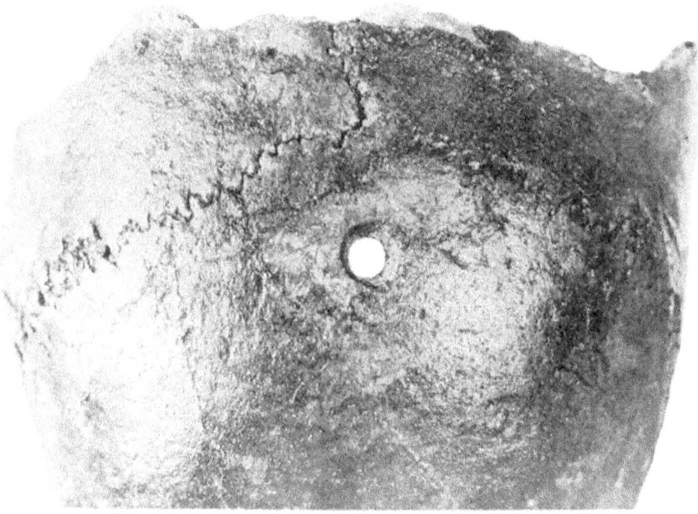

FIG. 2

PLATE II

Cranium with disk removed; perforation in the frontal bone. Flat Rock site, Wayne County, Michigan.

PLATE II

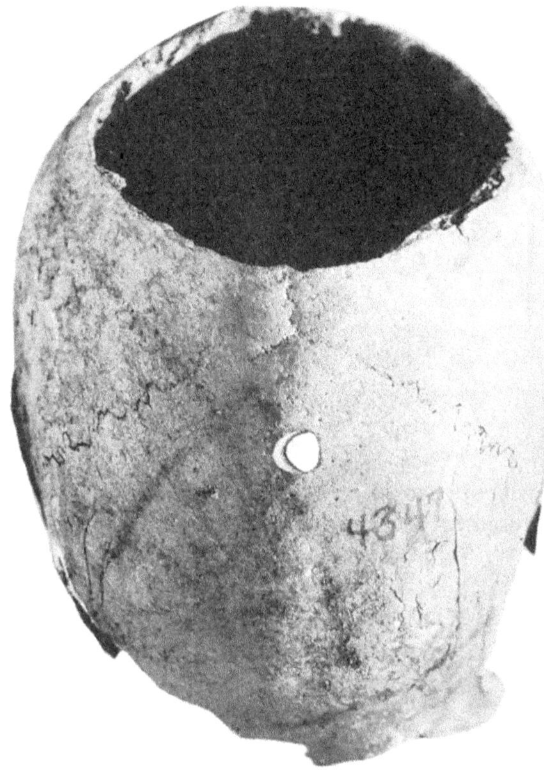

PLATE III

FIGS. 1-2. Two views of a cranium perforated near bregma and near the foramen magnum. From the Farmington site, Oakland County, Michigan.

PLATE III

Fig. 1

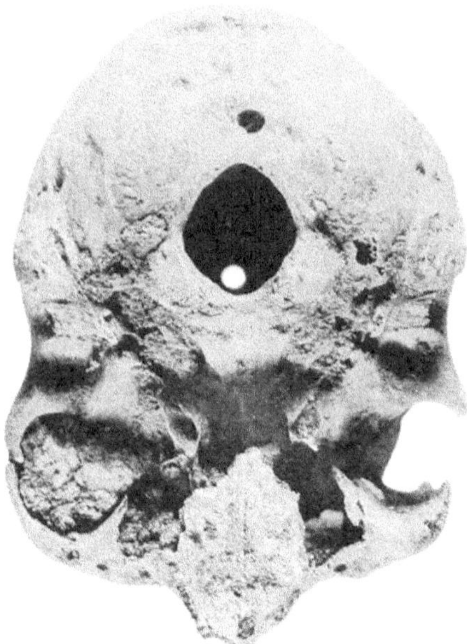

Fig. 2

PLATE IV

FIG. 1. Long bones with drilled holes. Farmington site, Oakland County, Michigan.

FIG. 2. Frontal bone with perforation. Younge site, Lapeer County, Michigan.

PLATE IV

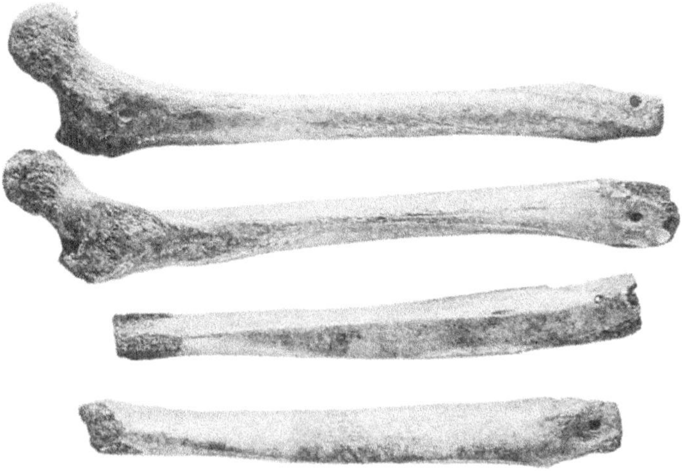

FIG. 1

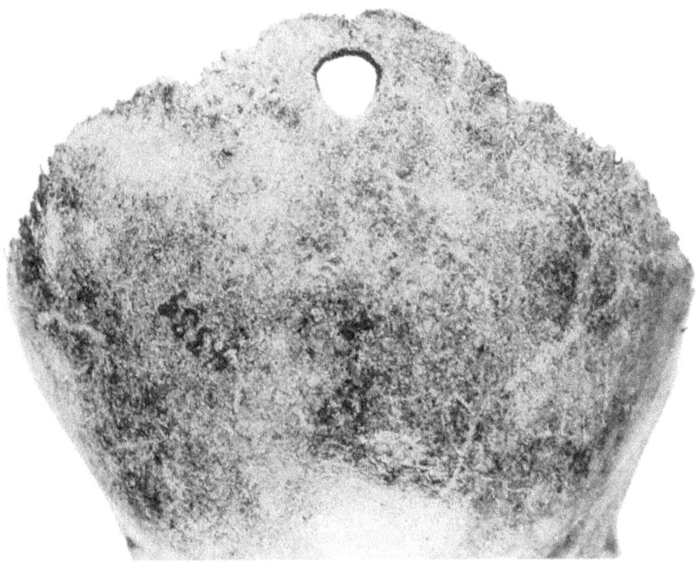

FIG. 2

PLATE V

Cranium with two perforations. From an unknown site in Michigan. Museum catalogue No. 4343.

PLATE V

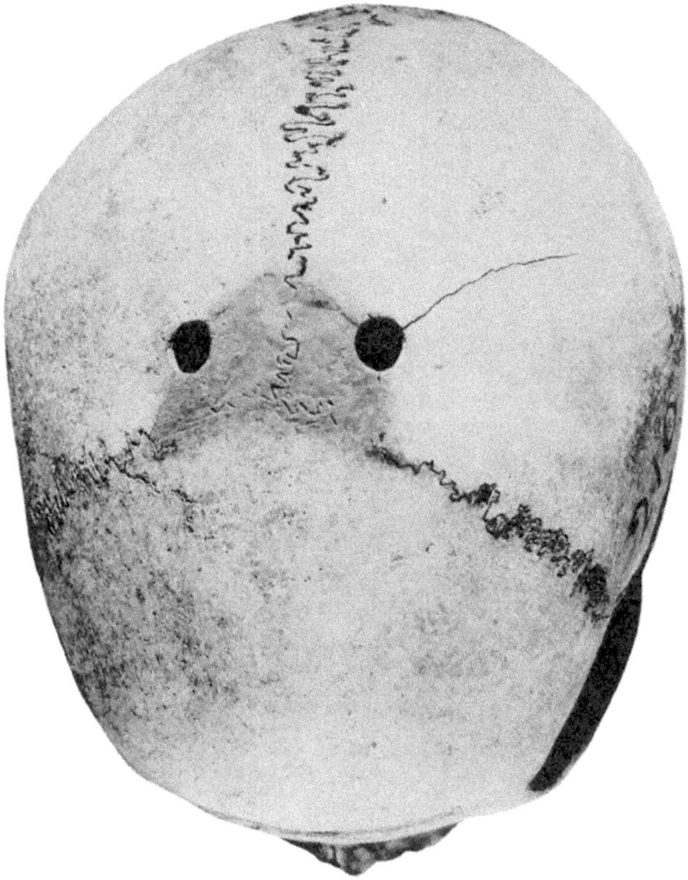

www.ingramcontent.com/pod-product-compliance
Lightning Source LLC
LaVergne TN
LVHW050022250826
846302LV00008B/66
9781949098587